Catherine was born in May 1729 as Sophia Augusta Fredericka, the daughter of an obscure German prince. There was nothing to suggest that one day she would become the absolute ruler of the Russian empire. But despite the lack of a really convincing claim to the throne, she went on to win for herself the reputation as a great enlightened monarch, corresponding with Voltaire and Montesquieu, instituting wide-ranging social reforms at home, and gaining for Russia the reputation of a progressive European power instead of a barbaric Asiatic one.

With the aid of more than fifty contemporary prints, engravings and maps, and key documentary extracts, Miriam Kochan offers a new assessment of Catherine's rise to power through the deposition of her husband Peter III in 1762; her problematical relations with the Russian nobility; her many lovers, from Gregory Orlov to Stanislaus Poniatowski (whom she made King of Poland); her schemes of aggrandisement which involved her in wars with Sweden and Turkey; the Pugachev rising; and she analyses how in her later years the ageing Empress felt slowly forced to surrender her reforming ideas, in the face of troubles at home and the shock-waves of the 1789 revolution in France.

This is a fascinating story of how, for more than 30 years, one remarkably gifted and intelligent woman confronted the immense challenges and temptations of absolute power.

Catherine the Great

Miriam Kochan

To Joanna

WAYLAND PUBLISHERS LIMITED

Wayland Kings and Queens

Charlemagne	Keith Ellis
Alfred the Great	Jennifer Westwood
Charles V	William Rayner
Henry VIII	David Fletcher
Mary Queen of Scots	Alan Bold
Elizabeth I	Alan Kendall
James I	David Walter
Charles I	Hugh Purcell
Charles II	Michael Gibson
Louis XIV	Christopher Martin
Peter the Great	Michael Gibson
Catherine the Great	Miriam Kochan
Napoleon I	Stephen Pratt
Queen Victoria	Richard Garrett
Wilhelm II	Richard Garrett

SBN 85340 421 6
Copyright © 1976 by Wayland (Publishers) Ltd
49 Landsdowne Place, Hove, East Sussex BN3 1HS
Text set in 12/13 pt. Photon Baskerville, printed by
photolithography, and bound in Great Britain
at The Pitman Press, Bath

Contents

1 An Empress Proclaimed

CATHERINE ALEXANDROVNA, wife of the Emperor of Russia, awoke with a start. The sun was streaming in through the French windows of her bedroom, catching the reflected glimmer of the sea of the Finnish Gulf not far away. But it was not the bright light that had awoken her: a figure was bending over her bed. She opened her eyes fully and sat up with a start at seeing the dark handsome face leaning towards her.

"Alexei," she gasped, "what is it?"

"Little Mother, all is ready for the proclamation. You must get up."

Without another word, Catherine threw back the silk sheets, hurried out of bed, and went into her dressing room. She hastily put on the black dress she had worn the day before – black because she was still in mourning for Empress Elizabeth who had died less than a year before.

Quickly, Catherine called her maid; the two women followed Alexei Orlov across the beautiful lawns of the royal palace of Peterhof. At the edge of the grounds, an open carriage was waiting for them. Alexei helped them in and, with a flick of the whip, urged the horses onwards towards St. Petersburg, capital of Russia. They had nearly reached their destination when, through the swirl of white dust raised by the horses' hooves, they saw another carriage approaching them. With a cry of delight, Catherine recognized its driver as her lover, Gregory Orlov, Alexei's brother. The change of vehicles was quickly made, and she continued the journey at Gregory's side.

Their first stop was at the headquarters of the Ismailov guards regiment, where Catherine had many

"Our entry into the city beggared all description. Countless people thronged the streets shouting and screaming, invoking blessings upon us and giving vent to their joy in a thousand ways, while the old and the sick were held up at open windows by their children to enable them to see with their own eyes the triumph that shone on everyone's face." *Memoirs of Princess Dashkov.*

Left Catherine in 1762, the year she became Empress of Russia.

friends. Here, she was greeted with noisy cheers. The soldiers rushed out to kiss her hands, her feet, the hem of her dress. Two of them fetched a priest with a cross. One and all swore the oath of loyalty to her as their new Queen. Led by the priest, and followed by the troops, they moved onwards, to the Semionovsky regiment where the same performance was repeated.

Quite a procession was following the carriage holding the slim woman in the black dress, by the time it reached the Kazan Cathedral in St. Petersburg. Here it was joined by the Preobrazhensky regiment and the Horse Guard. A bishop bearing a cross came out to greet her, to bless her as the new Empress of Russia, and to bless her little son and heir Paul Petrovich. Paul himself, however, did not appear on the scene until the next stage in the drama, when the colourful procession had moved on to the Winter Palace. A chubby boy of eight, he arrived still clad in pyjamas in the care of his tutor, Nikolai Panin.

Leaving her son with him, the new Empress continued on her triumphant journey. She had still to solve the most difficult question of her husband, Peter III of Russia. He was still, as far as he knew, Emperor. Now, mounted on a white horse and dressed in full guards uniform, Catherine rode at the head of an armed force to obtain Peter's abdication. As she left St. Petersburg, proclamations in the name of the "Empress Catherine" were already being issued.

Within twenty-four hours the Emperor Peter III was a prisoner of the new monarch. Within a fortnight, he was dead.

Overnight a new Empress had been made; an Emperor had passed into oblivion. How had these dramatic events come about? Who was this remarkable woman, who had quietly and unobtrusively seized the throne of one of the largest empires in the world?

Opposite page Peter III, Catherine's husband, in 1762 – the year in which he was deposed from the throne of Russia.

2 The Little Princess

2ND MAY, 1729, was not a happy day in the grey stone house at 1, Grosse Dornstrasse. Here, in the small German state of Stettin, lived Prince Christian Augustus of Anhalt-Zerbst. His sixteen-year-old wife, Johanna Elizabeth of Holstein-Gottorp, had given birth on that grey morning – not to the son and heir they so much wanted – but to a baby girl. They called her Sophia Augusta Fredericka. There was nothing to make them think that one day this small, puny German princess would be Catherine II, Empress of Russia.

Nothing about her suggested this glorious future. She was not beautiful or important or rich. In fact she was downright ugly as a young child and her parents were anything but well off. The most they could have hoped for was to marry their daughter to some minor European princeling of the same class as her father – and there were many of them in eighteenth-century Europe – who would not mind these things.

Nothing about her upbringing prepared her for her future career. When Sophia was seven years old, her dolls and toys were taken away and the serious business of living began. She did not mind very much; she had never cared for dolls. Instead she was given lessons: lessons in history, geography, religion. French and German she learned as a matter of course. Music she never learned, despite many attempts.

There was certainly nothing dull about her life. She was always travelling around Europe with her mother, visiting various members of her vast family at courts all over Germany. For Johanna Elizabeth was very well-connected. When Princess Sophia was ten years old she first met her second cousin, Charles Peter Ulrich of

"I watched Princess Sophia grow up and witnessed the progress she made in her studies . . . From her early youth, I merely observed in her a cold, calculating and serious disposition, but also one that was as far from being outstanding or brilliant as it was from folly, lightness or extravagance. In short, I formed the opinion that she would turn out a very ordinary woman . . ." *Report by Baroness von Prinzen, lady-in-waiting to Catherine's mother.*

Holstein, on one of these visits. He was then eleven, a pale delicate boy, though rumours were already flying about that he was a little too fond of alcohol. Hints were dropped that he might make a husband for the young princess of Anhalt-Zerbst, but they were always dismissed. Charles Peter would need a wife who could add to his wealth and position. Like her, there was nothing to show that his fortunes too would take a dramatic change. Yet only three years after this uneventful meeting, his aunt the Empress Elizabeth of Russia summoned him to St. Petersburg, made him heir to the throne, and baptized him into the Greek Orthodox Church with the name of Peter Fedorovitch. Elizabeth herself had no children; her nephew Charles Peter

"I knew that he was one day to become King of Sweden, and the title of Queen rang sweet to my ears, child though I was." *Memoirs of Catherine the Great.*

11

Right Empress Elizabeth of Russia, daughter of Peter the Great and aunt of Peter III.

would have to do. His mother, who had died shortly after his birth, had, like Elizabeth, been a daughter of the great Russian Czar, Peter the Great.

Empress Elizabeth had chosen her heir; now she must find him a wife. Imagine the excitement in Stettin when a letter arrived on New Year's Day, 1744, inviting the young Princess Sophia, then aged fourteen, to visit Russia with her mother. No-one found it hard to guess the reasons behind the invitation – least of all Sophia herself, who had been dreaming about crowns ever since she was seven. Had not her second cousin, Princess Augusta of Saxe-Gotha, married Britain's Prince of Wales? Her mother too could not have been greatly surprised. She had been very busy since Peter had gone to Russia, renewing her connections with the Empress Elizabeth and sending portraits of her young daughter

Left Catherine as a young girl, then called Sophia.

for her approval. Princess Sophia's looks had by this stage greatly improved.

Life for Sophia changed the minute the letter arrived. Her mother had never forgiven her for being a girl, but now she began to take an interest in her. The King of Prussia, mighty amongst European monarchs, made a great point of seeing and flattering the fourteen-year-old girl when the family were in Berlin.

And then it was time to go. The neighing horses stamped their feet impatiently outside the door, their breath steaming in the cold January air. Sadly, Sophia bid farewell to her father, whom she was never to see again, and she and her mother climbed into the carriage. The adventure which was to change Sophia Augusta Fredericka of Anhalt-Zerbst into Catherine II of Russia had begun.

3 Sophia becomes Catherine

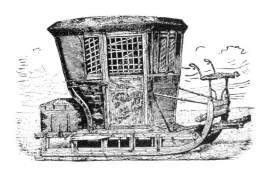

Above A Russian travelling sledge, of the type in which Catherine made her journey from Riga to Moscow.

> "I believe that the Crown of Russia attracted me more than his person. He was sixteen, quite good-looking before the pox, but small and infantile, talking of nothing but soldiers and toys." *Memoirs of Catherine the Great.*

IT IS NOT EASY to visit Russia today. Two hundred years ago it took the Princess Sophia six weeks from the moment that she and her mother stepped into their horse-drawn carriage in Germany until they finally stepped out at Riga in Russia. Even then, the journey was not over. They had to take sledges to St. Petersburg and then on to Moscow. By the end, Sophia's feet were so swollen she had to be carried. Her mother sustained a blow on the head when their sleigh bumped into a house on the way, but fortunately suffered no ill effects.

It was a totally different world they stepped into. Most of Russia's vast population were peasants – serfs who literally belonged to their noble masters. Sophia must have seen their wretched log cabins as she crossed the flat, snow-covered Russian countryside. She must also have spotted the magnificent palaces standing a little apart from the clusters of these huts, where the noblemen lived in fabulous luxury.

But even more sumptuous than the life of the eighteenth-century Russian noble was the life of the court of the Empress Elizabeth. It was this life that Sophia was now to enter. She had her first taste of it when she was given gifts of beautiful sable furs while still in Riga. Like any other fourteen-year-old girl, it was the clothes which impressed her the most. She always remembered the first time she saw the Empress in person: she was wearing a silver *moiré* dress with gold braid, and had a black feather in her hair amidst a mass of diamonds. Sophia herself wore a tight-fitting gown of rose *moiré* and silver for this important occasion.

The Grand Duke, the young Peter, was there to welcome his future wife. He was obviously delighted to

Его Императорское Высочество
Государь наследник благовѣрный Великій Княз...
ПЕТРЪ ѲЕОДОРОВИЧЬ,
Внукъ Государя Императора Петра Великаго.
S. Kaiserliche Hoheit der Großfürst
PETER FEODOROWITSCH
Kaisers Peter des Großen Enckel.

Left The young Peter III, dressed in armour. He spent a great deal of his time playing with his toy soldiers.

see her. He was only a boy himself – and young for his age at that – and very pleased to have someone of his own age to chatter and play with. He was particularly fond of playing with soldiers. He had had a rather miserable childhood, this Peter. Before going to Russia, he had been brought up very strictly by tutors whom he hated; and he had never liked Russia. He always thought of himself as a Prussian, worshipped the famous Prussian King, Frederick the Great, and never even tried to learn Russian or to please the Russian people over whom he would one day rule.

Sophia, on the other hand, tried very hard to please

Above Anna Johannovna, Empress of Russia from 1730 to 1740.

"As I was very gay by nature, it pleased me when I realized that I was daily winning the affection of the public who considered me an interesting, not un-intelligent child." *Memoirs of Catherine the Great.*

from the moment she set foot on Russian soil. She was very good at it. She had been trying to make people like her ever since she first realized that her mother had wanted a boy. She set out to learn Russian. She also worked hard to understand the Greek Orthodox religion which was the religion of the country. If she was to marry Peter, she would have to give up the Lutheran faith in which she had been brought up.

Sophia was converted to Greek Orthodoxy in the June following her arrival in Russia. It was a very elaborate ceremony, during which she was re-named Catherine. Everyone was impressed at the way she recited her confession of faith in pure clear Russian. She was led to the church by Empress Elizabeth herself, both of them dressed in scarlet and silver.

The next day, her engagement to Peter was formally announced. Under a solid silver canopy carried by eight major-generals, the Empress led Sophia (now Catherine) and the Grand Duke Peter to the church, where they exchanged rings. Catherine wrote that the one she gave him cost fourteen thousand roubles, the one he gave her, only twelve.

Catherine was showered with presents from the Empress to celebrate these occasions: a necklace and a diamond ornament on the first; Elizabeth's portrait framed in diamonds at the second. She was certainly managing to please so far.

The same could not be said of her mother, Johanna Elizabeth. After years of moving in her mother's shadow Catherine rather enjoyed the setbacks she suffered. She took pleasure in her right to walk before her mother at state occasions. She was pleased when people accused her mother of not looking after her properly when she fell ill.

But in the months before the wedding Empress Elizabeth made more serious charges against Johanna. She had heard that Johanna was acting as a spy for Germany. Elizabeth was furious. She could not send the mother home before the daughter's wedding. Catherine and Peter must be married as quickly as possible.

4 Love and Marriage

CATHERINE looked lovely on her wedding day. She wore a dress of shimmering silver cloth, which can still be seen today in the Kremlin Museum in Moscow. Peter did not look so beautiful. He had never been a handsome boy, and not even his white and silver costume could hide the recent smallpox which had left his face so horribly pitted. But this could not be seen by the crowds who lined the streets as the magnificent procession, glittering with jewels, drove to the Cathedral. Even the horses were covered in precious stones.

Empress Elizabeth was determined that this should be a wedding the like of which Russia had never seen. She sent enquiries all over Europe to find out how royal marriages were conducted there. The Empress, like her father Peter the Great, deeply wanted to make Russia a modern European state – not the medieval Asiatic land it had until recently been. Hence she adopted the customs and habits of European countries, especially France.

Catherine was very excited on her wedding day. This marriage was bringing her one step nearer to the crown of Russia. She was not exactly happy. She knew that she did not love, and could never love, her childish young husband. She also knew that he did not love her. He liked to play with her and chat to her. He was always telling her about his fondness for other ladies at the court. Even in these early days, Peter only thought of Catherine as a cousin and a friend.

As the years went on, the Empress Elizabeth grew rather angry with the young couple. She was always afraid that they were meddling in politics. She herself had seized power by violence. She always feared that

"In short, never did two minds resemble each other less than ours; we had nothing in common in our tastes, nor in our ways of thinking. Our opinions were so different that we would never have agreed on anything, had I not often given in to him so as not to affront him too noticeably." *Memoirs of Catherine the Great.*

someone else might overthrow her in the same way.

The Empress was also annoyed that Catherine did not become pregnant. More than anything else the Empress wanted a future heir to the throne. She tried all sorts of strange methods to cope with these problems. She did everything she could to force Catherine and Peter closer together. Every time one of them became friendly with anyone – man or woman, servant or courtier – that person was dismissed and sent as far away as possible. Catherine was forbidden to write letters, even to her parents (her mother had gone home right after the wedding). Most important, Elizabeth put a married couple, the Chogolovs, in charge of the pair. The Chogolovs were told to watch over Peter and Catherine carefully and report on their behaviour. The Empress also hoped that the example of the Chogolovs' domestic bliss would be infectious.

It made not the slightest difference to Catherine and Peter. They went more and more their separate ways. Each of them took lovers. Peter's favourite was a lady called Elizabeth Vorontsov. Catherine's first real love was a gentleman called Serge Saltikov. Not long after their affair began, nine years after her marriage to Peter, she found she was expecting a child. There was tremendous rejoicing both in the country and in the palace when the new heir to the throne, Paul, was born on 20th September, 1754. But Catherine wept alone. For the moment the baby was born, the Empress swept into the room and took the child away. After that, the young mother was not allowed to look after him and only saw him rarely.

Catherine felt even more unhappy and deserted. To console herself she began to read a great deal. She began to read very serious books, particularly by French authors of the movement known as the Enlightenment, like Montesquieu and Voltaire. This movement in eighteenth-century Europe was an attempt to solve mankind's problems by reason, not by religion and superstition as in the past. This started Catherine thinking a great deal about how a country should be

Left François Marie Arouet de Voltaire. Leader of the Enlightenment movement in France in the eighteenth century, his writings greatly influenced Catherine in the early years of her reign. This double portrait shows him both as a young and an old man.

"The Grand Duchess is romantic, ardent, passionate. Her eyes are brilliant, their look fascinating and glassy – the expression of a wild beast. Her forehead is lofty, and, if I am not mistaken, a long and terrifying future is written on it. She is prepossessing and affable, but when she comes close to me, I instinctively recoil, for she frightens me." *Chevalier d'Eon, Louis XV's secret agent quoted in Memoirs of Catherine the Great.*

Right Frederick the Great of Prussia. During the Seven Years' War between Russia and Prussia from 1756 to 1762, Peter III secretly hoped that Frederick would win.

"... To be general and drill sergeant on parade in the morning, to have an excellent dinner with a good bottle of burgundy, to spend the evening with his buffoons and a few women and to do whatever he was ordered by the King of Prussia – this was Peter III's idea of bliss. And this was, during the seven months of his reign, the pattern of his daily life which certainly inspired no respect." *Memoirs of Princess Dashkov.*

governed. She was also gaining a little practical experience of governing. Peter still had the title of Duke of Holstein, a small state in Germany. He did not enjoy the business of administering his kingdom and Catherine was very happy to help him in this.

But Peter's love for his duchy was as strong as ever. Nothing pleased him more than to march around in the uniform of a Holstein officer. At one point he shipped a whole detachment of Holstein guards over to Russia. One of his favourite amusements was to drill them on the parade ground. It was much more fun than playing with toy soldiers. Needless to say, the Russian people did not care for these foreign activities. They liked them even less when, in 1756, war broke out between Russia and Prussia (later known as the Seven Years' War). Peter made no secret of the fact that he hoped his idol, Frederick the Great of Prussia, would win.

5 An Emperor for a Husband

ELIZABETH OF RUSSIA lay dying. She was only fifty-two, but years of rich living had taken their toll. One question tormented her tortured brain: was her heir, the Grand Duke Peter, capable of ruling the country? She died on Christmas Day, 1761, without finding an answer.

Peter could hardly hide his joy at his aunt's death. Even at her funeral he could not behave decently. By first skipping ahead and then lagging behind in the solemn procession, he made things almost impossible for the gentlemen who were carrying his long, heavy, black train. Even before the funeral, he began to celebrate his title of Emperor Peter III. He gave great banquets and forced the members of the court to come to them. They had to obey him, but many of them were still red-eyed from weeping for the Empress.

Catherine, too, was worn out with tears. She dressed in deep mourning and kept a vigil over the Empress's body as it lay in state in the Cathedral. There was little else she could do except mourn during the early weeks of her husband's reign. The deep folds of her black gown hardly hid the fact that she was pregnant again. Her new lover, a handsome young guards officer called Gregory Orlov, was the father. Their little son was quietly born on 11th April, 1762.

The grief she showed at Empress Elizabeth's death won her much affection from the Russian people. They also felt sorry for her. Peter seemed to show his wife no affection at all. On the contrary, he made it quite clear that he intended to get rid of Catherine as soon as possible so that he could marry his mistress, Elizabeth Vorontsov. He missed no opportunity of insulting Catherine. He took away her jewels and gave them to

Above Gregory Orlov, Catherine's lover and father of her second son.

Elizabeth Vorontsov. He made Catherine attend dinners where Elizabeth was seated in the place of honour. At one such function, Catherine said she did not stand up to drink the toast to the Imperial family because she thought she was a member of it. Peter publicly called her a fool.

Meantime, Peter was offending Russian public opinion in more serious ways – especially in the Church and in the army. He had never hidden his lack of interest in the Greek Orthodox religion, which he had had to adopt when Elizabeth made him her heir. He rarely went to church, and when he did he behaved very rudely. Once, he is even said to have thumbed his nose at a bishop. Now he was in power, he announced that he would confiscate all the property of the Church (and the Church in eighteenth-century Russia had a vast amount of property). Instead, priests would be paid by the state. Needless to say, this did not make him very popular with them.

The army had never liked Peter's love for Prussia, their enemy. One of Peter's first acts after his aunt died was to sign a peace treaty with Prussia – and this at a time when Russia's army was close to conquering the enemy. In 1760, it had even entered the Prussian capital, Berlin. (Peter had gone into mourning at the time to show his grief!) Soldiers had fought and seen their comrades die for such a triumph: they were horrified suddenly to be told that the war was over, and to see their Emperor going out of his way to flatter Frederick the Great. They were even more horrified at being told to wear German-style uniforms. Then came the announcement that Peter had appointed his German uncle, Prince George of Holstein, head of the army.

By this time, the soldiers were feeling far from well disposed towards their new Emperor; they had no desire to support him in a new military campaign he was planning. This campaign was to be against Denmark. Peter wanted to march off straight away to win back from Denmark the small German state of Schleswig which was traditionally attached to his own Duchy of Holstein.

The army was not interested in Schleswig. They were

". . . I then saw that three equally dangerous paths opened up before me: *primo* – to share his Highness's fate, whatever it might be: *secundo* – to be exposed at any moment to anything he might undertake for or against me; *tertio* – to take a route independent of any such eventuality. But to speak more plainly, it was a matter of either perishing with (or because) of him, or else of saving myself, the children, and perhaps the State from the wreckage to which the moral and physical qualities of this Prince were leading us." *Memoirs of Catherine the Great.*

Left Peter III and Frederick the Great making peace at the end of the Seven Years' War, on 5th May, 1762.

23

Above Gregory Orlov, one of the leaders of the plot to overthrow Peter III in 1762.

not interested in Holstein. They were no longer even interested in Peter III as a ruler. Soon, mutterings were heard of a plot to overthrow him and put his wife Catherine on the throne. By June 1762, some thirty to forty officers were in the secret, supported by some 10,000 soldiers who were ready to act. Among the leaders of the conspiracy were Catherine's lover, Gregory Orlov and his four brothers. They were helped by an eighteen-year-old girl, with connections in high places and a great love for Catherine, the Princess Dashkov. On the morning of 28th June, 1762, they moved into action . . .

6 Peter III Deposed

PETER III did not stand a chance. He was caught unawares. He was quite outclassed by Catherine, the handsome Orlov troop and the other conspirators. When the news of the events of 28th June reached him, he was busy drilling his Holstein soldiers at Oranienbaum, a palace near St. Petersburg, in readiness for the campaign against Denmark. He rushed back to Peterhof but found the place deserted. He took a boat to Kronstadt, the naval base of St. Petersburg, hoping that the fleet would help him. But Kronstadt was already in the hands of Catherine's supporters. Emperor Peter III was not allowed to land.

In a state of confusion and dejection, he went back to the palace at Oranienbaum. Here, Alexei Orlov took him prisoner, and watched over his shoulder while he signed a paper of abdication. Then Alexei took him to Ropsha, a little estate also near St. Petersburg, where he was kept as a prisoner. Catherine did her best to make her husband comfortable. She sent him most of the things he asked for: his violin, his pet dog and his favourite black slave, Narcissus.

After this, no one really knows what happened. Reports reached Catherine, busy with the tasks of government in St. Petersburg, that Peter was ill. A doctor was sent. She heard he was better. Then suddenly, on 6th July, a note was brought to her from Ropsha. It was written by Alexei Orlov and said that Peter had died. He had been killed in a drunken fight with his guards the evening before. No one knew exactly who had killed him. Even today no one is absolutely sure. Was his death really an accident? Had it been ordered by Catherine, fearing he would remain a rival to the crown? Had

"What do you say to a Czarina mounting horse and marching at the head of 14,000 men to dethrone her husband? Yet she is not the only Virago in the country. The conspiracy was conducted by the sister of the Czar's mistress, a heroine under twenty! They have no fewer than two czars now in coops, that is, supposing the gentle damsels have murdered neither of them . . ." *Letter from Horace Walpole, 10th August, 1762.*

"My dear Lady! I swear by my life I know not myself how that misfortune happened. We are lost if you do not show mercy. My dear Lady, he is no more. But it never occurred to anyone, and how could it occur to us, to lift a hand against our Sovereign. But my Sovereign Lady, a misfortune happened. He started arguing at table with Prince Theodor. We did not have time to separate them before he passed away. We cannot remember what we were doing, but we are all guilty, every one of us, and worthy of death . . ." *Letter from Alexei Orlov to Catherine.*

Alexei acted on his own initiative to make certain that Catherine's position as Empress was secure?

The report of Peter's death came at an awkward moment for Catherine. On the very same day, 6th July, she had published Peter's abdication and her manifesto of accession. This stated that she had had to mount the throne because the Empire was in danger; the Church was threatened; the Russian army was suffering; the system of government was being overthrown. For the sake of the people of Russia, she had been forced to take power into her own hands.

The next day, she had to make another announcement, to say that the former Emperor Peter III had died of an internal haemorrhage. A post mortem had been held because Catherine wanted to prove to everyone that he had not been poisoned.

Left A medal struck on the accession of Catherine to the Russian throne in 1762.

Few tears were shed for Peter. But rumours about the way he had died flew everywhere, not only all over Russia but throughout Europe. Catherine did not feel secure. She went ahead as fast as she could with plans for her own coronation. On 22nd September, the great day dawned. In solemn procession, wearing a gown of silver cloth trimmed with ermine, and followed closely by her friend Princess Dashkov, Catherine moved towards the Kremlin Palace in Moscow. The high, jewelled Russian crown was placed on her chestnut-coloured hair, and as she was proclaimed Catherine II of Russia all the bells of Moscow rang out. They continued to ring, for the coronation celebrations went on long into the winter. Silver pieces were distributed among the people; there were balls and banquets, firework displays and parties of a magnificence that had never been seen before.

Catherine was truly Empress of Russia. But in her heart she never really felt the throne belonged to her. She could never quite forget that she had once been Sophia of Anhalt-Zerbst, a German princess, and had no legal right to the Russian throne. She knew, too, that a prisoner in the remote fortress of Schlusselberg had a far better claim to the crown than herself. He had been Ivan VI of Russia, thrown into prison when he was a baby by the Empress Elizabeth when she had seized power. In 1764, two years after Catherine's accession, when this innocent lad was 23 years old, he was murdered in a scuffle said to have taken place between his guards and some rebels who wanted to place him on the throne.

Ivan's death hardly increased Catherine's right to the Russian throne. But it did eliminate any competitors.

Left The coronation of Catherine in the Kremlin Palace in Moscow, on 22nd September, 1762. From a painting by Stephano Torelli.

7 Private Life

Right Catherine the stateswoman: here receiving the Ottoman Ambassador after her coronation.

CATHERINE settled down to work the minute she seized power. She had a vast territory to govern. Russia, even at the beginning of her reign, was vast. By the time she died, it was larger still. What is more, the ruler of Russia governed this great area practically alone. There was no elected government. The Russian monarch was an autocrat with complete power. She merely chose a small council of ministers herself, to help and advise her.

Right from the start Catherine took the business of governing very seriously. She got up at five o'clock every morning and worked solidly until ten. During those five hours, she received ministers, drafted laws, read through reports from all over the empire, wrote letters and so on. Only when she was satisfied that she had done all she could, would she go down to breakfast. Then

came prayers; to the end of her life, she continued to practise the Greek Orthodox religion she had been baptized into.

She often passed the time until lunch at two driving out in a coach or sleigh – depending on the time of year. Driving through the streets of St. Petersburg was a very fashionable pastime, when everyone exchanged greetings, and noted each other's dress, and companions. But Catherine went out without guards and very few attendants. She did not like to be saluted or greeted as Empress.

This desire for simplicity and privacy pervaded all her private life. After lunch, she withdrew to her own apartments until tea at five. Then, in the evening she might see a little company, though Sir John Harris, the British Ambassador to Russia, records that he often had supper alone with the Empress. They ate a very simple meal off a card table, without attendants.

Sometimes she liked to give small dinner parties for eight to ten people. At these, the lover of the moment usually sat on the Empress's right hand. For there was always a lover. Gregory Orlov, the man who had done so much to put her on the throne, lasted quite a long

Left Catherine's great sled, in which she would drive out to meet her people.

Above The palace of Tsarskoe Selo, Catherine's country palace.

time. In the early years there were rumours that she was going to marry him, but this never came about. In the end he was discarded and replaced by others. In fact, the role of lover to the Empress almost became a public appointment. Whoever he was, the incumbent was paid a large salary and given all sorts of honours and distinctions, together with his own private apartments close to the Empress's. When he was dismissed, he received expensive presents, usually an estate to live on and probably a title.

Sometimes the evening was spent playing cards. Catherine loved a game of whist, and she was a good player. On other evenings, she went to concerts or to the theatre. She was never very fond of music but the theatre she loved and did much to encourage it.

She took her love of privacy to an extreme when she went to stay at her beautiful country palace at Tsarskoe Selo. Once there, she dropped all formalities and treated her ladies-in-waiting as equals. She pinned on the wall: *Regulations to which all who enter therein must submit.* They began by stating: "They will leave their dignity at the door together with their hats and swords." Anyone who stood up as a mark of respect when Catherine entered a room had to pay a fine.

This was Catherine, the private individual – a woman who cared nothing for the trappings and show of power. Her main interest lay in exercising that power for the good of the country. For herself she wanted only a simple life.

Yet she lived this simple life within a court of magnificent splendour. Never had such glittering extravagance been seen before. Many contemporary observers have described the functions at the court: the jewellery and the gold everywhere; the diamonds given as prizes for games played. Firework displays of stupendous brilliance and complexity were held in front of the Winter Palace; dazzling arrangements of every conceivable colour and design transformed that already beautiful building into a fairyland. Fantastic fancy dress parties were held in which Catherine changed her costume at least three times in an evening, when orchestras played and troupes of dancers entertained the company throughout the night.

But whether the party was still going on or not, as the clock struck five in the morning the Empress would slip quietly away from the gaiety and go to her study. The day was beginning and the work of government had to go on.

Above The Winter Palace at St. Petersburg.

"Fourteen large rooms and galleries were opened for the accommodation of the masks; and I was informed that there were present several thousand people. A great part of the company wore dominos, or capuchin dresses . . . The Empress herself, at the time I saw Her Majesty, wore a Grecian habit, though I was afterwards told that she varied her dress two or three times during the masquerade . . ." *Richardson, Anecdotes of the Russian Empire (1784)*.

8 Catherine the Lawmaker

CATHERINE now had the chance to put her theories about government into practice. The years she had spent reading and thinking about the best way to govern were not to be wasted. Now she had the power, she could not wait to carry out her ideas.

One of her first ambitions was to reform Russia's legal system. The laws were in a terrible muddle and resulted in innumerable injustices, inequalities and confusion. As a first step Catherine summoned a "Commission for the Drawing up of a New Code of Law", usually known as the Legislative Commission. This was to contain representatives of all classes of society from all over Russia; even the peasants were invited to send delegates, though the Church was excluded.

To show the Legislative Commission the lines on which she wanted it to work, Catherine spent two years writing her *Nakaz* (Instructions) for its guidance. The *Nakaz* gave her a marvellous chance to set down her ideas.

These were very much the fashionable ideas of eighteenth-century Europe during the Enlightenment. The intellectual centre of the Enlightenment was in France and scholars like Voltaire and Montesquieu were at its head. All sorts of startling new ideas were being aired – all men were equal, all men were born free, all men had equal rights . . . These ideas seem very ordinary to us today. In the eighteenth century they were quite revolutionary.

In large bold handwriting, Catherine covered sheet after sheet of heavy white, gilt-edged paper with her version of these theories; she loved writing. Any action which might harm anybody or damage the community

Above Catherine's portfolio, in which she carried her State papers.

should be forbidden. All men must be equal before the law, and must obey it. But they must be free to do anything the law did not forbid.

On two points, though, Catherine did not follow these fine theories. Firstly, the *Nakaz* permitted the nobles to go on keeping peasants as serfs (though to be fair it discouraged any increase in this practice). Catherine did not really approve of the serf system, but she knew that abolishing it would be far too drastic a measure for the time. It would also make her very unpopular with the nobles, and she badly needed their

35

support. It was they, after all, who had placed her on the throne. However, nothing could have been more unequal than the relationship between the serfs and their noble masters.

Catherine felt much more strongly on the second point. All men might be equal, but she would still be an all-powerful autocrat reigning over all of them. She saw herself as an enlightened despot, ruling alone but by enlightened principles to bring about the greatest good for all her subjects. Russia was such an enormous country, she argued, that only one person with absolute authority could be strong enough to govern it.

This suited Catherine down to the ground. She was a natural autocrat at heart. Early on, she had found she disliked sharing the work of government with her husband, Peter III. She wanted nothing better than to hold absolute power and to rule alone. Enlightened despotism was in fashion at this period. Maria Theresa in Austria and Frederick the Great in Germany, both ruled autocratically but liberally over their countries. Catherine wanted to follow their example.

She also hoped that they would accept her as a European monarch. Russia still had the reputation of being a wild uncultured Asiatic country. Catherine had set herself a hard task in changing this image. The strange deaths of two heirs to the throne hardly made Europeans think of Russia as civilized. Catherine had to work extremely hard to convince them. The *Nakaz* was one of her first attempts in this direction. It was translated, published and distributed in many European countries, and on the whole it made a good impression.

Another method she used to draw closer to Europe was to correspond with leaders of European thought, like Voltaire and Diderot, as well as Frederick the Great himself. Letters flowed to and from St. Petersburg in which these illustrious personages exchanged ideas on liberal government.

And how was liberal government progressing in Russia at this time? Well, Catherine's Legislative Commission did meet. In all, more than five hundred

RUSSIANS

delegates gathered in the Kremlin in Moscow on 30th July, 1767. Six months later, they moved to St. Petersburg. But although the Commission went on meeting and discussing the problems of serfdom, merchants and nobles, and so on, for another year, it was dissolved without any reform in Russia's legal system being made. The five hundred or so members went home having achieved nothing.

Above A Western view of the relationship of the landowners and the serfs in Russia. It was this inequality that Catherine set out to break down in the *Nakaz*.

9 The Enlightened Despot

IT IS NOT quite fair to Catherine to say that the Legislative Commission achieved nothing. After all, it did bring together a very mixed crowd of delegates who would not otherwise have met. It was the first time such a gathering had ever taken place in Russia. The discussions about the points in the *Nakaz* put all sorts of new ideas into people's minds. The members of the Commission went back to their homes all over the country and talked about these revolutionary ideas to their friends. Even the lowest classes of peasants heard about them.

More concrete results of Catherine's enlightened views can be seen in her other actions. For example, she did a great deal for medicine in Russia, particularly in fighting smallpox. She had always been terrified of this disease, which was very common and very dangerous in her day. Her husband Peter III had been horribly disfigured by it during their engagement. Catherine herself was always imagining that she had caught it. When she heard of the preventive success of inoculation in Europe she invited Dr. Thomas Dimsdale, the British expert to come to St. Petersburg. In 1768, watched by an admiring crowd, Catherine was publicly inoculated. The Senate was so impressed by her bravery in undergoing the operation – and at the age of 40 – that it presented her with twelve gold medals and put up an inscription on Senate House stating: "She saved others to the danger of herself." That same year, Catherine gave the money to open a smallpox hospital.

Education was another of her great interests. Very soon after she had become Empress, she sent a Commission to Britain to take a look at schools and universities here and make suggestions for a new Russian

"267: You must add too to this, that two hundred years are now elapsed since a disease unknown to our ancestors was imported from America, and hurried on the destruction of the human race. This disease spreads wide its mournful and destructive effects in many of our provinces. The utmost care ought to be taken of the health of the citizens. It would be highly prudent, therefore, to stop the progress of this disease by the laws." *Instructions*.

Left Catherine presented her mandate to the chairman of the commission for drawing up the new regulations of 1767.

educational system. A new system was certainly needed. Most of the millions of peasants had never been to school and could neither read nor write. There were not even adequate schools for the nobility, though education was compulsory for the sons of noblemen. As for girls, hardly anything at all existed for them until Catherine opened two seminaries, one in Moscow and one in St. Petersburg, for the education of young ladies. All branches of education improved under her enthusiastic patronage. Schools for children of all classes of society were opened in provincial and district centres. Special schools were started for the sons of merchants; they encouraged them to travel abroad at the end of the course to see what trading methods were used in the West. The existing schools for nobles were improved and new ones founded.

The nobles and the merchants – the upper classes – did best out of both Catherine's educational and medical measures. In these early days, the new schools barely reached the poor peasants; and when they were ill, they much preferred to pray to the Virgin Mary than pay for a doctor.

Catherine also realized that Russia's vast rich lands were not being cultivated as well as they might be. One reason was that some areas were underpopulated. Catherine encouraged immigration of every sort. She even advertised in foreign newspapers inviting people to come and settle in Russia. On the whole, she did not mind what religion or nationality they had – itself a sign of her enlightenment. She hoped that they would teach the Russian landowners how to farm their land better; their old-fashioned and wasteful methods of agriculture was another reason for rather low production levels. In 1765 Catherine founded the Free Economic Society. One of its main tasks was to study the methods used in western Europe and to spread knowledge of them in Russia. Every year the Society ran an essay competition on a set agricultural subject.

Also with her eye on agriculture, Catherine ordered a regular population census to be taken, and asked for

"A hostel for foundlings was established, a school for the Academy of Beaux Arts, a school for noble young girls, one for the bourgeoises; pensions were granted to all those unfit to be employed, a bank was established in Astrakhan; a fund for widows was started, and a pawnbroker's was opened. A great deal of work was put into the reform of the laws and there was an impressive amount of building." *Catherine lists her achievements.*

Below Russian peasants. This illustration was drawn for an English
geography book in the eighteenth century.

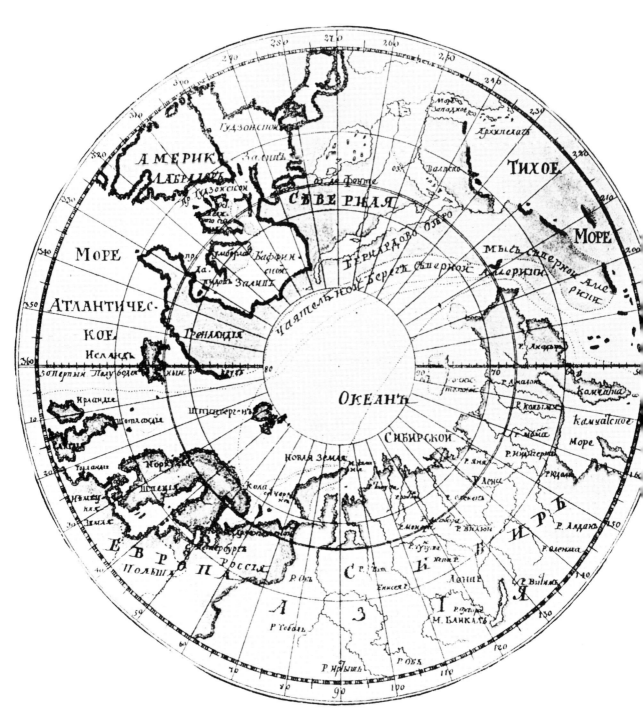

42

statistics to be published of prices, customs duties and imports and exports.

Her love of adding to the knowledge of Russia took other directions as well. She initiated all kinds of research into Russian history. She wanted to make collections of all the treaties Russia had ever signed and of old Russian manuscripts – until then hidden away in monasteries all over the country. She wanted all documents relating to the history of Russia to be carefully stored in the major libraries. She even wrote a history book herself. It was called *Pieces Relating to Russian History*.

Her intense interest in everything Russian extended to the geography of the country. Here again, she commanded research to be undertaken. Expeditions were despatched to every corner of the land to compile records about the earth and water there, the minerals, arts and trade, crops and animals – to mention just a few of the many topics covered.

Not only did Catherine enrich Russia's knowledge of itself. She filled its museums, art galleries and libraries by buying important scientific and artistic collections from abroad. Her own collection of pictures was priceless and can still be seen in the Hermitage Museum today.

Left A map of the countries in the polar region; this appeared in *A Brief Description of Sundry Voyages Along the Northern Seas*, by M. N. Lomonosov, published in 1763. This was one of the results of Catherine's keenness to explore and chart the vast land over which she ruled.

44

10 Russia and Europe

CATHERINE'S PLANS for Russia were not limited to its internal well-being. She also dreamed of making it a strong international power. She wanted it to be accepted as a political equal by all the large western nations. She hoped that it would play a full part in trade with other states.

At the end of the seventeenth century, the western world still thought of Russia as a land of savages. To them, it was governed from the strange Asiatic town of Moscow by weird men with long beards and long robes. Peter the Great had done a great deal to change this image. Among other things he had forced the nobles to shave off their beards, and he had founded a west-facing capital city, St. Petersburg. Catherine continued his policy. She went on trying to make Russia respected as a military and naval power; and to expand its territory, particularly its coastline.

To be able to trade freely, Russia needed access to large sea ports. One of Catherine's first moves after she came to the throne was to make sure that the four countries which divided Russia from the important Baltic sea were friendly to her. These countries were Esthonia and Livonia, which Peter the Great had already gained for Russia, Courland and Poland.

Catherine began on a small scale with the tiny Duchy of Courland. The Duke of Courland in 1762 was the son of the King of Poland. The country was very much under Polish influence. This did not suit Catherine at all. Using strong-arm methods of persuasion, which included sending Russian soldiers to Courland, she managed in 1763 to put a Russian on the throne and forced the previous Duke to pack his bags and leave.

> "At this time she had attained that degree of beauty which represents for every woman to whom beauty is given at all the climax of its development."
> *Poniatowski of Catherine aged 26.*

Left Peter the Great cutting off the beard of a Boyar. A contemporary cartoon.

Above Stanislaus Poniatowski, another of Catherine's lovers, whom she wanted to become King of Poland.

Pleased with this relatively easy success, she turned her mind to greater things. The situation in Poland was ripe for action. The King of Poland had died in 1763. A new king had to be elected – for Poland had the unusual system then of choosing a king by voting in the Diet (parliament). Catherine wanted someone to do Russia's bidding. She had just the man for the job – a young Polish noble called Stanislaus Poniatowski. He had been in love with Catherine for the past eight years ever since he had been her lover in 1755. (He comes between Serge Saltikov and Gregory Orlov in time sequence.) Then, she had been the Grand Duchess, swept off her feet by the handsome cultured young European. Now, she was Empress and had moved on to greater things. But she still kept in touch with Stanislaus, and he still kept his great love for her and still hoped one day to marry her.

He had no desire whatever to be king of Poland. Reluctantly, only to please Catherine, he agreed to stand as candidate. To make sure he won, Catherine sought the help of Frederick the Great, who also did not want to see Poland a strong country on his northern borders. Between them the two great monarchs, once enemies, now allies, used the threat of their combined strength, plus Russian money and Russian troops, to have Stanislaus elected king of Poland in 1764.

It was not a happy position. Stanislaus had been right to think twice about accepting it. In 1768, civil war broke out in Poland. Russian troops were again to the fore. But before the conflict was settled, Catherine found a much bigger problem on her hands.

She was faced, in fact, by an attack on a quite different front. Turkey, on her southern border, was an ancient enemy of Russia. Now, Turkey took advantage of Russia's involvement in Poland to declare war on Russia and to attack from the Crimea. Catherine was taken by surprise. Apart from anything else, some of her best troops were busy in Poland. Not until the spring of 1769 was Catherine ready to act properly. Then she struck against Turkey in two quite unexpected directions. Firstly, she attacked the Balkan peninsula, where her armies

Above The Russian fleet destroying the Turkish fleet off the Dardanelles on 7th July, 1770.

won brilliant victories, capturing Jassy, the capital of the Turkish province of Moldavia, and Bucharest, capital of the province of Wallachia. Secondly, she had in the interim been building up a very impressive fleet which suddenly appeared in the Mediterranean and destroyed the Turkish fleet at Chesme off the island of Chios.

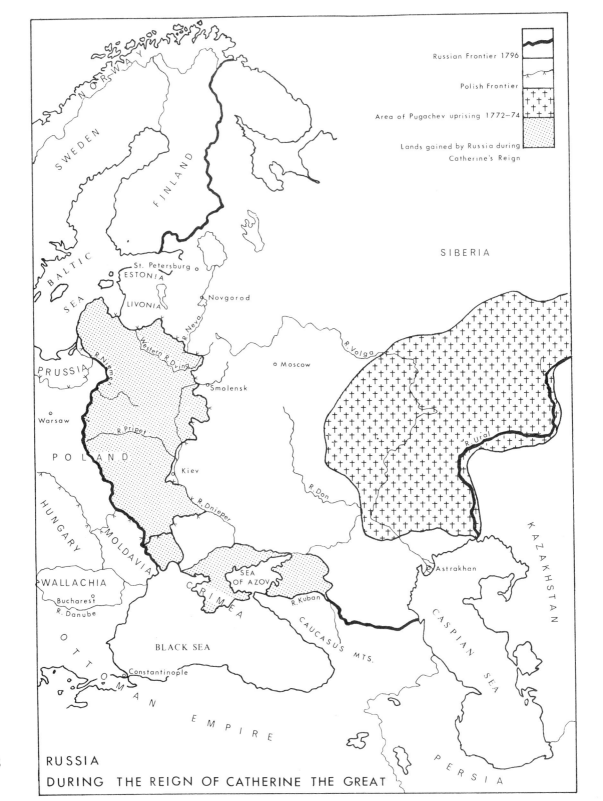

	Russian Frontier 1796
	Polish Frontier
	Area of Pugachev uprising 1772-74
	Lands gained by Russia during Catherine's Reign

SWEDEN

NORWAY

FINLAND

SIBERIA

BALTIC SEA

St. Petersburg o

ESTONIA

LIVONIA

o Novgorod

R. Neva

R. Volga

Western R. Dvina

PRUSSIA

R. Niemen

o Moscow

R. Ural

Smolensk

o Warsaw

R. Pripet

POLAND

Kiev

R. Dnieper

R. Don

HUNGARY

MOLDAVIA

o Astrakhan

KAZAKHSTAN

WALLACHIA

CRIMEA

SEA OF AZOV

Bucharest

R. Danube

R. Kuban

CAUCASUS MTS.

CASPIAN SEA

OTTOMAN

BLACK SEA

Constantinople

EMPIRE

PERSIA

48

RUSSIA
DURING THE REIGN OF CATHERINE THE GREAT

Never again would the West be able to sneer at Russian military or naval force. Catherine was gloriously victorious. She celebrated her triumph with a solemn mass at the Cathedral of Peter and Paul in Moscow. It was at this point that a new dream was born in her mind. She began to see herself as governing a vast empire from Constantinople.

The other European states were not so pleased. Did they really want to see Turkey disappear from the map as a great power? Would they like to see Catherine ruling triumphantly from Constantinople? Even Catherine's friend, Frederick of Prussia, was none too happy at the prospect. It was Frederick in fact, who found the answer to the problems of both Poland and Turkey. It was one which suited him too. He had always wanted to annexe the piece of Poland adjoining the Prussian border. He therefore suggested that he should take this slice; Russia should take another slice, and in return should begin peace talks with Turkey.

Catherine agreed. After the first two startling successes, the wars in Poland and Turkey had begun to drag, and she also heard rumblings of trouble at home. In 1772, therefore, what is called the first partition of Poland took place. Stanislaus remained King, but of a kingdom stripped of a quarter of its territory. Russia gained some valuable land as a result. She gained still more when in 1774 she finally signed the treaty of Kuchuk-Kainardji with Turkey.

Russia was at peace with the world but Catherine's dream of possessing Constantinople seemed temporarily unattainable. Later events proved that she had by no means discarded it.

"Her hair was black, her skin a dazzling white and vivid red; she had large blue, round, very expressive eyes, very long black lashes, a Grecian nose, a mouth which seemed to ask for kisses. Her arms and shoulders were surpassingly beautiful; she had a tall, graceful figure, and her walk was very agile though full of nobility; the sound of her voice was pleasant, and her laugh as joyous as her temperament."
Poniatowski of Catherine aged 26.

11 The Nobility

CATHERINE had been happy enough to accept the treaty of Kuchuk-Kainardji. Her enthusiasm for the Turkish adventure had for the time being subsided. She had other things on her mind. She had troubles far closer home, in Russia itself, where a major revolt broke out.

As we have seen, Russia was sharply split into two social classes: the nobles and the serfs – the relatively tiny upper class and the vast lower stratum. This lower class was now in revolt – to the extent that Catherine in St. Petersburg was terrified for her life. But the reasons for the revolt can only be found in the way of life of the upper orders.

Catherine was in a way to blame. Despite all she had said and written in her *Instructions* at the beginning of her reign about all men being equal, she had always favoured the nobility. She had to. After all, it was the noble guards regiments who had put her on the throne. If she displeased them, they could just as easily force her off.

Indeed, Catherine's reign is often known as the "golden age of the nobility". Never before and never since had the Russian nobles lived in such luxury and possessed such great power. The Russian aristocracy at this period was not like the British. It did not depend on heredity, on being passed down from father to son. Peter the Great had started a system whereby membership of the nobility was based on service to the state. Anyone could become a noble if he worked his way up in the ranks of the army, the navy or the civil service. When he reached a certain level, he entered the noble class. He then had two very important privileges: he was the only person in Russia (except the Empress) who

"360: Nobility is an Appellation of Honour, which distinguishes all those who are adorned with it from every other Person of inferior Rank." *The Instructions.*

Left A nobleman and his wife driving out in Moscow.

could own land and serfs. This was Peter the Great's system of a state to which every member gave service. The noble served the state in the army, navy or civil service. The serf served the state by working the land for the noble.

One of the first things Catherine's unfortunate husband Peter III had done, during his brief reign, was to free the nobles from the need to serve the state. Catherine confirmed this freedom. Only a few weeks after being proclaimed Empress, she also declared that she would protect "the noble proprietors in their lands and properties . . . Because the well-being of a state, in accordance with the Laws of God and all the laws of the people, requires that all and everyone shall remain upon his estate and shall be assured of his rights, we decide to

Left A Boyar, or Muscovian lord.

preserve to the *pomeshchiki* (landowners) the right to their estates and properties, and to keep the peasants in necessary obedience to them."

The duties had been taken away, but the privileges remained. The Russian nobles made full use of them. They used the land not only to feed themselves and their vast households, but also to supply every conceivable luxury. Otherwise, they did not bother with it very much. Essential supplies were not the only ones transported from their country estates to their magnificent mansions in St. Petersburg. Waggons loaded with rich and exotic fruits and vegetables filled the road. The nobles' attitude to their land, and absence from it most of the year in St. Petersburg, were major reasons why Russian agriculture was so backward. Even Catherine's

"New Economic Society" did not help it much.

The nobles exploited their serfs in a similar way. They had so many of them that they filled both town and country houses with servants. But these servants cost them nothing. They could use them to satisfy their slightest whim. If they suddenly felt like building an ice palace on their estates, they could immediately set hundreds of serfs to work and the palace would arise from nowhere overnight. They had their own orchestras made up entirely of serfs. They had theatres in their houses, staffed with whole companies of serf actors. They had dancing companies and operatic groups, all to perform for their private amusement.

Western visitors to Russia were staggered by the number of servants that appeared at the ring of a noble's bell. They were also amused at how the rough and ready Russian nobles tried to appear European. Everything French was particularly fashionable. Among themselves, they talked French as much as possible. They hired European tutors to educate their children. Catherine herself set the fashion by employing the Swiss philosopher La Harpe to teach her grandsons, Alexander and Constantine. They had their food cooked to French recipes. They filled their beautiful stone houses with western furniture, ornaments, carpets. They dressed in western fashions imported from France at enormous expense.

But they never really succeeded in obtaining more than a thin veneer of European culture. Inside, they were still the heirs of their uncouth uncultivated Asiatic ancestors.

"There is not a Bell in Russia except to the Churches, but if a fair one gently calls, four or five footmen are ready in any ante-chambers to obey her summons . . ." *The Russian Journals of Martha and Catherine Wilmot* (*1803–8*).

Opposite page The reception of serfs by a Boyar. Serfs had to pledge silent obedience to their masters, who could do with them what they liked.

12 The Serfs

WHEN SHE BEGAN her reign Catherine meant to do something to improve the life of the serfs. At least, she said she did.

Perhaps she just wanted to make a good impression on the countries of the West. Perhaps she really meant it, but when she came face to face with the facts of life in Russia and understood how strongly the nobles felt about serf-owning, she found it impossible to do anything. In fact, during her reign, the serfs reached the lowest level of social and economic degradation they had ever known. What is more, their numbers were growing. This was partly because Russia was conquering new territory, partly because Catherine was always giving enormous presents of land and serfs to reward her favourites and supporters.

The system of serfdom which tied each peasant family to certain land (and remember, only the crown, the Church and the nobles had the right to own land) had first started in order to make sure that the land was properly cultivated. Otherwise the Russian peasant had a habit of wandering off from one place to another whenever the fancy took him. By Catherine's reign, the peasant was so dependent upon his master (and most of the millions of serfs belonged to nobles), that he could only move from one estate to another if he had written permission. As one can imagine, this was seldom given. And this was by no means the only control the noble had over his serf. He could make him work for him in any way, for as long as he liked. He could even make him marry when and whom he wished. To cap it all he could (and did) sell him if he had no further need of him, or if he needed to raise money. Advertisements appeared

"He can sell him wholesale or retail. This is not said as a joke: for circumstances may be such that the daughter is sold apart from her mother, the son apart from the father, and, it may be, the wife separated from her husband." *Radischev, Description of My Estate.*

Left Two Russian peasants.

regularly in St. Petersburg or Moscow newspapers announcing that serfs would be put up for auction, together with animals. Here is a typical example:

"For sale – domestics and skilled craftsmen of good behaviour, *viz.* two tailors, a shoemaker, a watchmaker, a cook, a coachmaker, who may be inspected and their price ascertained in the 4th district, Section 3, at the proprietor's own house, No. 51. Also for sale are three young racehorses, one colt and two geldings and a pack of hounds, fifty in number, which will be a year old in January and February next."

Sometimes the animals fetched better prices than the serfs. Manpower was valued cheaply by the eighteenth-century Russian nobleman.

The household serfs – those who the lord decided should serve in his house in the country or in St. Petersburg – were among the worst off. They owned nothing of their own, and had to do the most varied jobs. They could be togged up in footman's livery and made to wait at table. They could be made to sing in an opera or dance in a ballet or a hundred and one other fantastic things to suit the lord's sometimes eccentric pleasure.

The condition of the ordinary serf was little better. True, he had his own patch of land to cultivate and his own house to live in. But this house was usually nothing but a wretched log hut. It generally only had one room in which all the family lived and slept together with any animals they were lucky enough to own. This room had one main item of furniture: an enormous stove. Round this, they all huddled for warmth during the bitterly cold Russian winter.

As for the peasant's own patch of land, only if he had a good master did he have time to cultivate it properly. The lord could make him work on the noble estate for as many hours as he liked every day. The serf could only till his own soil to grow food for his own family in his spare time.

And there were other hardships the serf had to endure. He might be made to do all sorts of other duties,

Above A village near St. Petersburg, showing the rough wooden huts where the serfs lived.

like post duty, or carting wood from the forest for the lord, driving a sleigh over the snow-covered roads from the country to the St. Petersburg mansion. Every village also had to select a certain number of serfs for military service in the army. This was dreaded beyond all else. Apart from the sheer dangers of battle – thousands of serfs were killed in Catherine's military campaigns – it also meant no less than twenty-five years away from home and family for the miserable victim.

Did the peasant have any protection at all from the demands of the noble? In theory, he had to be allowed enough time to get his own work done. The law also stated that the serf must not suffer ruin through his lord's treatment. In return, he had to give his master silent obedience. In practice, only the silent obedience could be enforced. Hardly any attempt was made to restrain the landowner during Catherine's reign. He was able to give free play to his pleasures and whims.

"In Part Twelve, an officer has for sale a sixteen-year-old girl, formerly belonging to a poor house, who knows how to knit, sew, iron, starch and dress a lady. She has a nice figure and pretty face." *Advertisement in Russian newspaper (1797).*

13 The Pugachev Rising

CATHERINE was not worried. She had just heard the news that the peasants in the Ural area of Russia were in revolt. Peasant revolts were not uncommon at this period – not surprisingly, given the conditions in which the serfs lived. There were minor revolts right through the early years of Catherine's reign. The local land-owners or the army never had much trouble putting them down.

So when in 1771 she heard of this revolt by one Emilian Pugachev, she dismissed it as a "vile comedy" in her letters, and talked sarcastically of *ce marquis de Pougacheff*.

This Emilian Pugachev was a Cossack from the River Don area. The Cossacks had once been a warlike nomadic people and, though they had by now settled down, they still retained their basic character. They made fine soldiers. Pugachev himself had served in the Russian army in the fighting against Poland and Turkey. He had also served one or two terms in prison for various offences.

Now, in 1771, he reappeared on the scene claiming to be Peter III, Catherine's murdered husband. He had not, he said, actually died, as his wicked wife had announced. Instead, he had escaped in the nick of time. Now he had come back to help his suffering people. Pugachev set himself up with a magnificent court, a new Queen, an heir, and all the trappings of royalty. From here, he issued a stream of proclamations.

The peasants were only too happy to believe that their murdered king had returned. They were simple folk ready to believe anything, and the ideas that Pugachev was voicing were very attractive to them. He was

"... We are moreover persuaded that our faithful subjects will justly abhor the imposture of the rebel Pugachev, as destitute of all probability, and will repel the artifices of the ill-disposed, who seek and find their advantage in the seduction of the weak and credulous, and who cannot assuage their avidity but by ravaging their country, and by shedding of innocent blood." *Catherine's manifesto against Pugachev, 12th December, 1773.*

Left Emilian Pugachev, leader of the peasant uprising in 1771.

expressing all the thoughts that had been hatching in their own minds for some years. In the first place, the peasants always believed that when the real Peter III had freed the nobles from their obligation to serve the state, he had also meant to free the serfs from their obligation to serve the nobles. Pugachev, alias Peter III, announced that when he regained power he would do just that. "You, such as you are," he pronounced, "I enfranchise you, and give eternal freedom to your children and grandchildren . . . You will no longer work for a lord, and you will no longer pay taxes . . . When we have destroyed their enemies, the guilty nobles, each man will be able to enjoy a life of peace and tranquillity which shall endure for hundreds of years."

How could the down-trodden peasants resist such a pleasant prospect? Pugachev played on all their other grievances. He reminded them of the thousands of peasants who had been killed in Catherine's Polish and Turkish wars. He attributed a recent cholera epidemic to the anger of God at Catherine's actions.

The peasants flocked in their masses to him. And it was not only they to whom his message carried a strong appeal. Pugachev had chosen well in deciding to launch the revolt in the Urals. It was not only his fellow Cossacks here who joined his band. The Urals were also the main centre of Russian industry (still in a very early and undeveloped stage), with iron works, salt mines, silk factories. The industrial serfs who kept the wheels of this industry turning were treated even worse than the ordinary peasants. They slaved in appalling conditions often hundreds of miles from their homes and families. They too swelled Pugachev's ranks.

By November 1773, Pugachev's army had grown to quite a size. It was also quite well trained. The Cossacks taught the unskilled peasants and factory workers how to fight. When the rebels laid siege to the town of Orenberg, Catherine could no longer pretend that this was some minor, unimportant uprising which she could afford to ignore. "I fear that this business is going to end in many hangings, and how I hate them . . ." she wrote.

"Our Lord Jesus Christ deigns to desire, through Holy Providence, to free Russia from the yoke of servile toil, a toil, I tell you, which is known the world over." *Pugachev, 1774.*

64

She sent in her army to quell the revolt.

But Pugachev still advanced. More and more people flocked to his banner. As they swarmed across the countryside, they burned, looted and sacked every noble estate they came to. They murdered every nobleman they met and raped every noblewoman. The nobles in their path fled terrified to nearby Moscow for refuge. Panic grew. It reached its peak when the rebel troops captured the large city of Kazan and burned it to the ground. And still Catherine's army was powerless.

Not until July, 1774, did it win its first battle against Pugachev. After that, victory for the imperial army came fast. The rebels at last began to withdraw, and disintegrate into small groups. Many of them, tired and dejected, trudged home. Pugachev himself was captured, brought to Moscow in a cage and executed. Catherine refused to let him be tortured, as was the practice of the day. She had always disliked torture. In this respect, at least, she stuck to her enlightened ideas.

The revolt was over. Pugachev was dead. But Catherine had had a bad fright. Never before had her power been so openly and seriously threatened. This bloody episode had shown only too clearly what a stark division separated rich and poor in Russia, a division which could only end in even greater violence.

"You yourselves know how Russia is being used up and by whom: the nobility owns the peasants, and although it is written in the law that they are to treat them like their children, yet they look on them merely as slaves, and lower than their dogs."
Pugachev, 1774.

Left The capture of Pugachev in the Urals in 1775.

66

14 Family Matters

THE FIRST HALF of the 1770s were not all times of trouble for Catherine. In fact 1773 was marked by a particularly happy event. Her son Paul, then nineteen years old, was married.

Catherine and Paul had never got on very well. Their relationship had started off badly. The Empress Elizabeth had taken the baby away from his mother the moment he was born. Elizabeth looked after him completely by herself. When she died, Paul was eight years old. Catherine had only seen him occasionally up to that time, and felt little love for her son. She left his tutor Nikolai Panin in charge of him, and mother and son led separate lives.

Catherine was quite happy with this state of affairs. She wanted to keep her son in the background, out of the business of running the country. She never forgot that Paul's claim to the throne was far better than her own. He was, after all, recognized as Peter III's son (even if some people had doubts on the subject). Catherine was determined that there should be no question of a rebellion deposing her in his favour.

Paul on the other hand always remembered the events leading up to Catherine's coronation. He blamed her for his father's death. In his eyes, nothing she ever did was right.

But in 1773, for the first time, mother and son were united in happiness. There were nothing but smiles at the magnificent wedding celebrations. Catherine had been looking around for a wife for Paul since 1767, and had asked a Danish diplomat friend to keep his eyes open for someone suitable in Europe. "I do not wish for princess from a very important house," she wrote to

left Paul Petrovich, son of Catherine.

Right A caricature of Paul Petrovich, illustrating his unpopularity with the Russian people.

him, "I want a girl who would know herself *raised* when she becomes Grand-Duchess."

Events followed their normal course – normal at least for royal marriages. The whole process that once brought Catherine herself to Russia was being enacted again. Another obscure German princess was being borne from insignificance to greatness.

A suitable princess was duly found. In fact three princesses were found, for the Landgrave (ruler) o

Hesse Darmstadt had three daughters, none of them too stupid, none of them over-intelligent. Portrait miniatures of all three were sent to Catherine, who then invited the whole family to St. Petersburg. Paul was allowed to choose which of the three girls he fancied. He selected the middle daughter Wilhelmina. In no time at all she had become the Grand-Duchess Nathalie. "She is charming and affectionate," Catherine wrote. "I feel very pleased and my son is quite in love."

She did not go on feeling pleased for long. Nathalie may have been charming but she began to take far too great an interest in politics. Worse still, she encouraged Paul to demand a great part in governing the country. Under Nathalie's influence, Paul wrote a lengthy memorandum about his ideas which he sent to his mother.

Catherine ignored it. It did not endear her towards the young couple. She only thawed three years after the wedding when she heard that Nathalie was pregnant. More than anything else, Catherine wanted an heir to the throne. She was at Nathalie's bedside constantly when the moment of birth drew near. Tragically both mother and baby died. Catherine's grief was intense.

But Catherine had to have an heir. Five months after Nathalie's death, Paul was married again, this time to Princess Sophia-Augusta of Wurtemburg who became the Grand-Duchess Marie Fedorovna. This time, the outcome was much more satisfactory. Two sons were born, Alexander in 1777, Constantine in 1779. They were followed by several little girls as well as another son, Nicholas.

Catherine was not interested in the later children, but she took Alexander and Constantine over completely (just as Elizabeth had assumed complete control of Paul some twenty-three years earlier). She devoted careful thought to their upbringing and, like any other fond grandmother, found tremendous pleasure in their childish achievements. She even designed a special baby-garment to dress them in. When they were older, she wrote story books and histories for them to read.

"My desire is to bring Constantine to the throne of the Great Eastern Empire." *A Will made by Catherine in 1792.*

"The two principles in approaching the education of a prince are, in my opinion, to induce in him beneficence and respect for the truth. This makes him lovable in the eyes of God and men." *Note by Catherine.*

15 Love and Conquest

CATHERINE NAMED her adored grandsons Alexander and Constantine. The names reflected the dreams that filled her head during the 1770s. Alexander she wanted to succeed her as head of the Russian Empire – but of one as vast as that of Alexander the Great centuries before. Constantine she hoped would rule from the ancient Byzantine city of Constantinople.

For Catherine was embarking on a scheme of conquest on a massive scale. Moreover, she had a partner in

Below Constantinople (now called Instanbul); Catherine hoped that one day her grandson Constantine would rule an empire from here.

her dreams. Once more she was in love. Her new lover was no handsome young prince. By all accounts, Gregori Potemkin was nothing to look at. He was enormously tall, enormously strong, and he had only one eye. How he lost the other, no one quite knew, perhaps it was a duel with the Orlov brothers, or an eye infection which was not treated in time. Potemkin was not even young; he was already thirty-four when the affair began, ten years younger than Catherine.

But despite everything, Catherine loved him more dearly than she had loved anyone before or ever would again. She wrote letters to him whenever they were apart – even for an afternoon.

"The trouble is," she wrote, "that my heart is loth to remain even one hour without love; it is said that human vices are often concealed under the cloak of kindness and it is possible that such a disposition of the heart is

> "I wish to be preferred to all the former ones, to make you understand that no-one has ever loved you as much as I, and as I am the work of your hands, I wish that my repose should also be the work of your hands; that you should find joy in being kind to me, that you should try everything for my consolation and find consolation in me for the great work you have to accomplish, because of your high calling." *Letter from Gregori Potemkin to Catherine.*

Left Gregori Potemkin, the favourite of all Catherine's lovers.

Right A coin depicting Gregori
Potemkin.

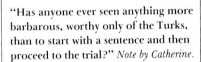

"Has anyone ever seen anything more
barbarous, worthy only of the Turks,
than to start with a sentence and then
proceed to the trial?" *Note by Catherine.*

more of a vice than a virtue, but I ought not to write this
to you, for you might stop loving me or refuse to go to
the Army fearing I should forget you, but I do not think
I could do anything so foolish, and if you wish to keep
me for ever, show me as much friendship as affection,
and continue to love me and to tell me the truth.''

Potemkin had served in one of the Guards regiments
that had helped to put Catherine on the throne in 1762.
On that occasion, he had been rewarded, as many others
had been, with a small estate. Later, in 1769, he had
fought in the Turkish war and distinguished himself by
his courage. It was while serving on the Turkish front
that he had received a message from Catherine sum-
moning him back to St. Petersburg . . .

And so their love began, and very soon their plans to
conquer Turkey.

First, Catherine decided, she must make friends with

Above The taking of Ochakov under Potemkin during the war in the Crimea with Turkey.

Austria. Austria, after all, owned the land adjoining Turkey's possessions in Europe. Catherine approached Emperor Joseph of Austria who was usually quite sympathetic towards her. They were both enlightened despots and got on well together. Joseph gladly paid a state visit to St. Petersburg in 1780 to discuss matters.

In 1782 Catherine outlined her plan for expelling the Turks from Europe and sharing out their land. First she wanted the Russian frontier to be pushed west to the River Dniester. Then the Turkish provinces of Moldavia, Bessarabia and Wallachia in the west were to be made into a separate kingdom of Dacia with Gregori Potemkin as king. Finally, she hoped to found an empire for Constantine with its capital at Constantinople. Austria's share of the spoils was to be Serbia, Herzegovina and Dalmatia.

Joseph of Austria was attracted by the plan, if

Above The ruins of Fort Nicolas, Sevastopol, in the barren wastes of the Crimea.

staggered by the Empress' ambitions.

But nothing could be done too soon. Potemkin was in a hurry to act but Catherine pointed out that a great many preparations had still to be made.

Meantime, while he waited for Catherine to give him the go-ahead, Potemkin and his troops moved into the Crimea. The Crimea had been left in Turkish hands by the treaty of Kuchuk-Kainardji. Now, in 1783, Potemkin managed to occupy it quite easily. He at once began reconstructing the area, fortifying and resettling it. And most important, he built or rebuilt two major naval ports: Kherson and Sevastopol.

16 Triumph
and War

THE 1780s saw Catherine and Potemkin once again with their heads together, planning another grandiose scheme. They were no longer lovers, but they were still the firmest of friends. Potemkin ruled supreme at court. It was said that he not only guided Catherine's policies, he also chose most of her lovers.

What they were planning now was a triumphal procession by the Empress to the newly developed lands of the Crimea.

On New Year's Day, 1787, the guests invited to join this expedition began to assemble in the Winter Palace. They included the French Ambassador to St. Petersburg and the British envoy, for this scheme was designed to impress the whole western world. Catherine was only disappointed that her grandsons Alexander and Constantine were not able to come. Their parents (who had not been invited) sent a message to say they were suffering from a mild attack of smallpox.

Left The Winter Palace, where the party assembled before Catherine's triumphal journey through the Crimea.

Above The Pechersk Monastery in the port of Kiev.

On 14th January the party was ready to depart. Fourteen great sleighs and between one and two hundred lesser sleighs left St. Petersburg and sped over the icy roads of Russia. The imperial sleigh bearing the Empress and her retinue was drawn by thirty horses; it was so large that it could be divided into three sizeable rooms.

By 9th February they had reached the port of Kiev. Here they were joined by a strange unshaven figure, dressed in a flowing robe. It was Gregori Potemkin. He was going through a mystical phase (once he had thought of being a monk) and was staying in a local monastery. The party had to stay in Kiev for several months waiting for the ice to break on the River Dnieper. Not until 1st May did the gaily painted boats sail off down the river, its banks lined with cheering crowds. On the way, Stanislaus Poniatowski, Catherine's old lover and now King of Poland, joined those on board. He was soon followed by Emperor Joseph of Austria.

The party was complete by the time it reached Kherson, where it passed under an arch bearing the name of the city in Greek. The story of Alexander the Great was still much in Catherine's mind. At Kherson she launched three battleships in the new harbour. Her pleasure was only marred by the appearance on the horizon of a Turkish flotilla. The next and final stop was Sevastopol, newly fortified and with forty warships lying at anchor in the bay.

Soon the time came to return. The party gradually broke up. At Kharkov, Catherine bid good-bye to Potemkin, bestowing upon him the title of Prince of Tauris and showering him with gifts. She came home to find Moscow in the grip of famine. Another shock soon followed. Turkey, already annoyed by the treaty of Kutchuk-Kainardji and Russia's seizure of the Crimea, was alarmed by the show of Russian strength during the Crimean trip. It declared war on Russia.

Catherine was not ready for war, at least not yet. It is said that she burst into tears when the news reached her. However, with typical strength of mind she quickly pulled herself together. It was she who forced Gregori Potemkin back into the fight when he became depressed at Russia's first disaster of the war. Potemkin wanted to throw up the struggle when the new Russian fleet was almost wiped out by heavy gales off Sevastopol. Later, he won back his reputation through several notable vic-

"At the entrance of every village her Majesty's *cortège* must be met by inhabitants dressed in their best. Married women must be decently and cleanly kerchiefed and girls are to have flowers in their hair. Nobody in unseemly or tattered clothes, still less in a state of inebriety, is to be seen anywhere . . ." *Instructions for procedure to be carried out along Crimean route.*

"They have already spread a ridiculous report that villages of cardboard have been distributed along our route at intervals of a hundred leagues, that paintings of vessels and cannon and cavalry without horses are displayed." *Letter from Prince de Ligne, a member of the party.*

tories, but he was growing more and more moody and unpredictable at this time.

After that, the story of the Turkish war is mainly one of successes for Russia. But victory itself was a slow and painful process. This was partly because some of the Russian troops had to be taken away from the Turkish front and sent northwards. Here, Russia's old enemy Sweden had taken advantage of the situation, and also attacked. In 1790 the Swedish fleet got as far as Kronstadt and the sound of cannon was even heard in St. Petersburg. Panic spread like wildfire in the city but Catherine sat unperturbed in the Winter Palace, reading.

She was right. Sweden was soon defeated and a peace was signed. But Catherine had lost her appetite for war with Turkey. All she wanted now was peace. Everything seemed to be going wrong for her. Her ally, Joseph of Austria, had died and Austria was out of the war. The recent outbreak of revolution in France (1789) and the flight of Louis XVI and Marie Antoinette had shaken her considerably. Britain and Prussia were ganging up against her to prevent her becoming too strong.

In 1791, Catherine signed the Peace of Jassy with Turkey. She gained some new land in the east but none of her great dreams was realized. The Kingdom of Dacia never materialized. The city of Constantinople remained in Turkish hands.

In 1791, too, she suffered a loss even greater than that of her dreams. Gregori Potemkin died of malaria while on a mission in Moldavia. "My pupil, I may say my idol, the Prince Potemkin, has died," she wrote.

Left The fall of the Bastille during the French revolution, 1789. Catherine was afraid that the echoes of revolution would one day reach Russia.

Left The execution of Marie Antoinette at the climax of the French Revolution, 1793.

17 The Lonely Autocrat

CATHERINE HAD CHANGED over the years. No longer was she the bright-eyed ambitious girl who read the works of Montesquieu and Voltaire; no longer the enthusiastic enlightened young monarch and author of Instructions for a new Legislative Commission. The ageing Empress had become a frightened woman.

The first great blow to her ideals had been struck by the Pugachev revolt as early as the 1770s. She had realized then, perhaps for the first time, the violence of which her adopted nation was capable. She was terrified that the Russian people could not seem to tell the difference between liberty and licence. How ever could she govern a country of serfs by enlightened methods?

It was the revolutionary movement which began in France in 1789 that ended any pretence Catherine had to being an enlightened despot. To many people, the French revolution seemed the logical – if violent – outcome of the ideas of the Enlightenment, of the rights of man. Here was the overthrow of the old autocratic monarchy, and the rise of a new democratic government.

To Catherine it seemed like death to herself and her régime. She identified herself with the hapless Louis XVI and Marie Antoinette of France. They had had to abandon their throne and flee for their lives. Later, in 1793, they were sentenced to death by a tribunal of the people, and publicly executed. This terrible fate must never happen to her. Revolutionary fever must not infect Russia.

She hastily cut off all contact with France in case the fever spread. In 1790 all Russians in France were ordered home. After 1791, French diplomatic represen-

"481: Nothing renders the crime of high treason more dependent upon the arbitrary interpretation and will of another than when indiscreet words are the subject of it." *The Instructions*.

Left A portrait of Catherine by M. Shibanov, painted in 1787.

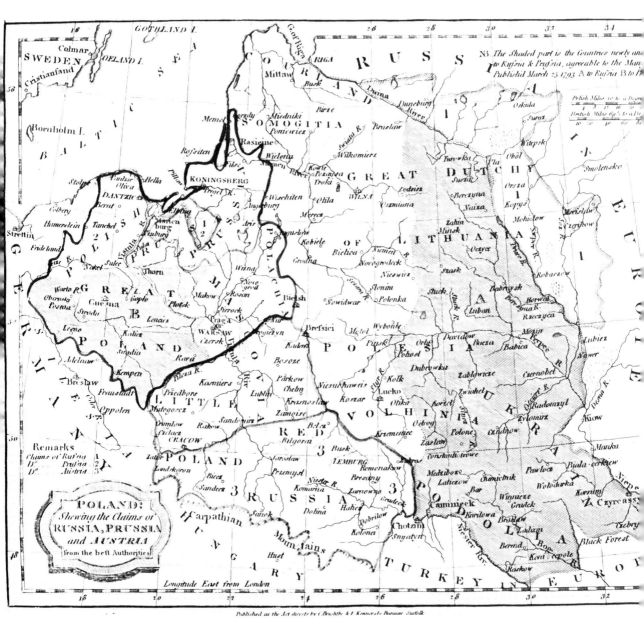

Above A map published in 1793, showing the claims of Prussia, Russia and Austria to the lands belonging to Poland. These claims resulted in the second partitioning of Poland in 1793.

"I am waiting the time when it will please you to exonerate in my mind those philosophers and others who have taken part in the revolution."
Catherine writing to Grimm.

84

tatives were no longer received at the Russian court. In 1793, Catherine finally broke off diplomatic relations with France and deported all French citizens in Russia – unless they would forswear revolutionary ideas.

At home, too, she began looking for anything that could even remotely be called "revolutionary". Any criticism of her régime became suspect. Books that dared to criticize Russian society were banned and their authors sent to Siberia. The victims included people like Alexander Radischev who had written a book called *A Journey from St. Petersburg to Moscow*; Denis Fonvizin, a playwright; and Nicholai Novikov, a bookseller and printer.

All were men of noble familes. They formed a loose group sometimes called the "conscience-stricken gentry". For the first time, nobles in Russia began to hold a mirror to their own country and see many things that were wrong with it. Why should a few people like themselves be well-off and live in comfort, while the mass of the population lived and died miserable serfs?

Catherine would stand none of this sort of talk. All down the margins of Radischev's book she wrote "stupid! venomous! untrue! dangerous!" There must be no question of criticism of the country reaching the dangerous masses. She took strong action against the nobles concerned.

On the other hand, she understood how much she depended on her nobles to keep the unruly masses in check. In 1785 she had already issued her Charter of the Nobility, to bind the nobles to her side. The Charter gave them many new privileges and confirmed their old ones.

Catherine's actions abroad show how far the enlightened despot had yielded to the reactionary autocrat. Over the years, a reform movement had grown up in Poland. It called for a more democratic *régime*, and freedom from Russian influence. Catherine, scenting another revolution like the French one, quickly sent in her troops in 1792, and after some vicious fighting broke up the movement. In 1793, the Polish Diet was

forced to accept a second partition of Poland. This gave Russia more land, but at the price of finally losing for Catherine the last shreds of any reputation as an enlightened monarch.

Nor did the Polish reformers and patriots take this lying down. They rebelled against the Russian forces occupying their country. The Russian army retaliated. Prussia greedily sent in soldiers to help. It was only a question of time before victory was theirs. In January 1795 Poland as a political entity ceased to exist. Russia, Prussia and Austria sat down and, in a third partition of Poland, split up the remaining territory between them.

Stanislaus Poniatowski, King of a non-existent country, was out of a job. He came to live in the same city as Catherine, his early love. He settled down in a mansion in St. Petersburg.

Left Stanislaus Poniatowski, who was deprived of his Polish Kingdom in 1793.

18 The End of an Era

THERE IS NOTHING romantic about growing old. By the time she was sixty, Catherine's chestnut hair was snowy white. She wore too much rouge on her cheeks, but her blue eyes were sharper and brighter than ever. She had put on a lot of weight over the years and nowadays wore long, flowing, eastern-type robes to conceal her rotund figure. She was not very tall, and was a little tubby, but somehow she always kept her dignity. People who met her say she always gave a great impression of majesty when she entered a room.

These were not happy years for Catherine. She went about less and less in public. Her legs were causing her pain, and walking was difficult. Orlov had gone. Potemkin was dead. There were fewer and fewer people left who had supported her during her period of triumph. She felt very much alone.

Without the diplomatic Potemkin to find her lovers for her, she was also rather at a loss. At the age of 61, Catherine took to her bed a lad of 22 called Platon Zubov. She fell madly in love with him. She was like a girl again. "I have returned to life like a fly that the cold had benumbed," she wrote. Platon was not however a particularly admirable character. He was very young (not much older than Catherine's own grandsons), spoilt, selfish, arrogant. He knew nothing, and cared less, about all the vicissitudes of Catherine's reign. He had no great feeling of loyalty towards her. He was only out for what he could get. But he remained "in office" for five years – until her death.

As she neared the end of her life, Catherine thought more about who should succeed her. She had always

Left A late portrait of Catherine by G. B. Lampi.

Right Alexander I, grandson of Catherine and Emperor of Russia from 1801 to 1825. Catherine's son Paul succeeded her to the throne on her death in 1796, but he was widely hated, and in 1801 was murdered by officers of the Russian Army. Alexander succeeded him in the same year.

hated the idea of her own son, Paul, becoming Emperor of Russia. She had not brought him up to govern the country. She had never given him any say in state affairs. She always intended her eldest grandson, Alexander, to follow her. Alexander had been given the sort of education suited to a future monarch. On several occasions, she mentioned her wish to arrange matters in this way. Yet something always stopped her. She died before she had taken any decisive action.

Her last months were marked by a grave disappointment. She had found wives for Alexander and Constantine. Now she had arranged a brilliant match for their sister Alexandra. The whole court, arrayed in splendour, with the Empress seated gloriously on her throne, waited the arrival of the young bridegroom, King Gustav IV of Sweden, so that the formal betrothal could take place. He never turned up. A hitch to do with Alexandra's religion had occurred at the last minute. Wretchedly, Catherine tottered from the court. That night she suffered a minor stroke. It was September, 1796.

But she seemed to recover quickly and resumed her normal life. On 6th November she went into her private room as usual. Hours passed. She did not emerge. Finally, the door was broken open. Catherine was found lying on the floor unconscious. She died the next day.

When she was young, Catherine had written her own epitaph. It ran as follows:

"Here lies Catherine II, born at Stettin the 2nd May, 1729. She went to Russia in 1744 to marry Peter III. At the age of fourteen, she made the triple resolution to please her husband, Elizabeth and the nation. She neglected nothing to achieve this. Eighteen years of *ennui* and solitude gave her the opportunity to read many books. Enthroned in Russia she desired nothing but the best for her country and tried to procure for her subjects happiness, liberty and wealth. She forgave easily and hated no-one. Tolerant, undemanding, of a gay disposition, she had a republican spirit and a kind heart. She made good friends."

520 . . . We think and esteem it Our Glory to declare 'That We are created for our people' and for this reason we are obliged to speak of things just as they ought to be. For God forbid that, after this legislation is finished, any nation on Earth should be more just; and, consequently, should flourish more than Russia; otherwise the intention of our laws would be totally frustrated; an unhappiness which I do not wish to survive." *The Instructions.*

Principal Characters

Alexander (1777–1825) son of Paul I, grandson of Catherine. As Alexander I, Emperor of Russia, 1801–25.

Alexandra, Grand Duchess (1783–1801), daughter of Paul, granddaughter of Catherine.

Christian Augustus, Prince of Anhalt-Zerbst, Catherine's father.

Constantine (1779–1831), son of Paul, grandson of Catherine.

Dashkov, Princess (1773–1810), friend of Catherine, sister of Peter III's mistress.

Elizabeth I (1709–61), Empress of Russia 1741–61.

Frederick the Great (1712–86), Emperor of Prussia.

Ivan VI (1740–64), infant Czar, deposed by Elizabeth I.

Johanna Elizabeth of Holstein Gottorp, Catherine's mother.

Joseph, Emperor of Austria (1741–90).

Nicholas (1796–1855), son of Paul, Emperor Nicholas I (1825–55).

Orlov, Count Alexei (1737–1808), one of the five Orlov brothers, instrumental in placing Catherine on the throne.

Orlov, Prince Gregori (1743–83). Another Orlov brother and Catherine's lover.

Panin, Count Nikolai (1718–83), tutor to Paul.

Paul Petrovich (1745–1801), son of Catherine and Peter. Later Emperor Paul I, 1796–1801.

Peter the Great (1672–1725). Emperor of Russia.

Peter III (1728–62). Originally Charles Peter Ulrich of Schleswig Holstein. Catherine's husband. Emperor of Russia, 1761–62.

Poniatowski, Prince Stanislaus (1732–98), Catherine's lover and last King of Poland.
Potemkin, Prince Gregori (1739–91), Catherine's lover.
Pugachev, Emilian (1726–75). Don Cossack rebel leader.
Radischev, Alexander (1749–1802), conscience-stricken gentry author – wrote *A Journey from Moscow to St. Petersburg*. Banished to Siberia by Catherine.
Saltikov, Serge. Catherine's first lover.
Vorontsov, Elizabeth (1739–92). Peter III's mistress.
Zubov, Prince Platon (1767–1822). Catherine's last lover.

Further Reading

Almedingen, E. M. *Catherine the Great* (Hutchinson, 1963).

Anthony, Katharine *Catherine the Great* (Jonathan Cape, 1931) – a romantic description of Catherine's life and loves.

Kochan, Miriam *Life in Russia under Catherine the Great* (Batsford, 1969) – a lively account of the social background to Catherine's reign.

Maroger, Dominique (Ed.) *The Memoires of Catherine the Great* (Hamish Hamilton, 1955) – Catherine's own memoirs, containing a detailed account of her daily life up to the age of 30.

Oldenburg, Zoe *Catherine the Great* (Heinemann, 1965) – A biography of Catherine concentrating on the years before she became Empress.

Table of Dates

Index

Picture Credits

The author and publisher wish to thank those who have given permission to reproduce illustrations on the following pages:
Mansell Collection, *frontispiece*, 13, 28, 32, 37, 59, 70, 76, 88; Mary Evans Picture Library, 11, 20, 21, 52, 55, 64, 78, 80 86; Novosti Picture Agency, *jacket back*, 6, 9, 16, 24, 38, 50, 82, 90; Radio Times Hulton Picture Library, 22, 29, 35, 42, 47, 56, 84. The remaining illustrations are the property of the Wayland Picture Library.
The illustration on the jacket front is reproduced by gracious permission of Her Majesty the Queen.